SQL Demystified

A Beginner's Roadmap to Data Retrieval and Management

Kaushal Mehta

ARCCHIE
www.arcchieonline.com

SQL Demystified

A Beginner's Roadmap to Data Retrieval and Management

Editor: Shambhu
Production Manager: Gaurav Mutreja
Cover design by Freepik and Vecteezy
Formatting & Indexing: Rahul

First Edition: Apr-2025
Reference: 2501236
Published by Arcchie Publications

ISBN-13 (paperback): 978-81-979768-0-3
ISBN-13 (eBook): 978-81-979768-1-0

Published by ARCCHIE PUBLICATIONS, Greater Noida, U.P. -201 306
and Printed at Repro India Ltd., Mumbai

www.arcchieonline.com

DEDICATED TO

My parents who have been a guiding light in my life.

- Kaushal Mehta

ACKNOWLEDGMENT

Writing **SQL Demystified** has been a deeply fulfilling journey—one that I could not have completed without the support, inspiration, and encouragement of many wonderful individuals.

First and foremost, I would like to express my heartfelt gratitude to Dr. Gaurav Arora—a friend, mentor, and a constant source of inspiration. His thoughtful insights, motivating words, and belief in this vision helped steer me through many pivotal moments of this writing process. Thank you for being the spark that set this journey in motion.

A special thanks goes out to the amazing team at Arcchie Publications. Your professionalism and commitment to quality have been truly outstanding. I'm especially thankful to Shubham, GM, and Sowmya for their dedication, enthusiasm, and tireless support throughout every stage of bringing this book to life. Your collaborative spirit helped shape raw content into a polished, reader-friendly resource.

Finally, to the readers—whether you're a beginner curious about databases or an experienced professional revisiting foundational concept, thank you for picking up this book. I hope it serves not just as a guide but as a companion on your learning journey. May it fuel your curiosity, deepen your understanding, and encourage you to explore the boundless world of data.

Thank you all for being part of this journey.

- Kaushal Mehta

ABOUT THE AUTHOR

Kaushal Mehta is an Associate Professor at Bhai Parmanand DSEU Shakarpur Campus-II, bringing over 15 years of rich academic and industry experience to the classroom. A passionate educator and lifelong learner, Kaushal has dedicated his career to empowering students with the knowledge and skills required to thrive in the ever-evolving world of technology and data.

With a strong foundation in computer science and database systems, he has guided countless learners—from undergraduates to working professionals—in mastering complex concepts through clarity, patience, and practical application. His teaching philosophy revolves around simplifying the intricate and making learning engaging, accessible, and relevant to real-world challenges.

Beyond the classroom, Kaushal is a contributor to curriculum development, academic mentorship, and innovative learning practices. SQL Demystified reflects his commitment to breaking down technical subjects into digestible, meaningful insights for beginners and enthusiasts alike. This book is an extension of his mission to make high-quality education more approachable and impactful.

As a respected voice in academia, Kaushal continues to inspire a new generation of tech-savvy thinkers, problem-solvers, and future innovators.

PREFACE

In today's data-driven world, the ability to understand, retrieve, and manipulate information stored in databases is not just a technical skill, it's a foundational one. Whether you're working in business, healthcare, education, or technology, chances are that Structured Query Language—better known as SQL—plays a role behind the scenes.

The book SQL Demystified demonstrates in a simple goal: to make SQL approachable for absolute beginners. Over the years, as an educator and mentor, I've seen students and professionals alike struggle with the intimidating syntax, jargon, and complexity often associated with databases. This book is my attempt to change that perception.

This is not a textbook that overwhelms with theory. It's a practical roadmap guided journey that starts from the very basics and gradually builds up to more advanced concepts. It takes you through real-world scenarios, hands-on SQL scripts, and case studies inspired by practical business environments like GlobalMart and TechRetail Corp. Each chapter is designed to help you not only understand how SQL works, but also why it matters.

You'll learn how to:

- Understand relational database structures
- Write and optimize SQL queries
- Join tables and analyze data
- Create views, stored procedures, and subqueries
- Manage transactions and concurrency in multi-user environments
- Apply your skills to solve real-world data problems

Whether you are a student preparing for exams, a job seeker adding SQL to your toolkit, or a curious learner entering the world of data for the first time—this book is for you. No prior programming experience is required. All you need is curiosity and a willingness to learn.

Let's embark on this journey of learning together.

What's Inside This Book

Chapter 1: Introduction to Databases sets up foundation of databases. It covers the basic components of a database system and the role of SQL in managing and querying data.

Chapter 2: Getting Started with SQL guides you through the essential foundational concepts operations starting with setting up the ground to work with SQL.

Chapter 3: Data Retrieval Techniques delves into advanced methods for querying and filtering data using column aliases, the DISTINCT clause, and operators like CONCAT and Q. This chapter delves into efficient data retrieval strategies to refine your SQL queries.

Chapter 4: SQL Joins – Combining Data from Multiple Tables explores the various ways to join multiple tables to produce data.

Chapter 5: Subqueries and Nested Queries demonstrates queries and use of sub-queries and queries to retrieve the data.

Chapter 6: Views and Stored Procedures details Views and Stored Procedures and describes the usage to retrieve the data.

Chapter 7: Transactions and Concurrency Control Discover the pivotal roles of core database objects using transactions.

Chapter 8: Advanced SQL Functions SQL functions are powerful tools for data manipulation and extraction. This chapter explores various types of SQL functions and their applications, enabling you to effectively query and analyze your database.

For Whom This Book Is Intended

This book is written with the beginner in mind—whether you're stepping into the world of databases for the first time or looking to strengthen your foundational knowledge in SQL. SQL Demystified is ideal for:

- **Students** pursuing computer science, information technology, or data science courses need a clear, practical understanding of SQL concepts for academic success.
- **Job seekers and fresh graduates** preparing for technical interviews or aiming to boost their employability with a must-have skill in the data-driven job market.
- **Working professionals** from non-technical backgrounds who interact with data and reports and wish to confidently work with databases without relying entirely on developers.
- **Beginner programmers** and analysts who are new to relational databases and want to learn how to query, manage, and analyze data effectively using SQL.

- **Educators and trainers** are looking for a classroom-friendly resource that balances theory with hands-on practice and real-world use cases.
- **Anyone curious about data** and eager to learn how modern systems store, retrieve, and manage information using structured queries.

Maximize your Learning Experience with this book

To start with this no prior knowledge is required. Readers can learn as they go chapter-by- chapter:

To set up the system, reader should have following on their machine:

- SQL IDE: This is a well-known IDE used by developers all over the world. It has an easy-to-use interface and a toolkit with formatting features, object browsers, SQL worksheets, and data modelers. It also has a very intuitive SQL editor with a testing mechanism. ***https://www.oracle.com/database/sqldeveloper/technologies/download/***

Tools: Tools are best for coping with different database development, management, reporting, analysis, and monitoring operations. They cover a wide range of functions, thus enabling you to achieve the best result and ensure flexibility. Few common tools are mentioned below:

- Toad for SQL Server ***https://www.quest.com/products/toad-for-sql-server/***
- Microsoft SQL Server Management Studio Express: ***https://learn.microsoft.com/en-us/sql/ssms/download-sql-server-management-studio-ssms?view=sql-server-ver16***

Errata

At **ARCCHIE Publications**, we are committed to delivering the highest-quality content in all our publications. We follow best practices to ensure the accuracy of our content to provide our readers with indulgent reading experience. We believe and understand that our readers are our best judges, and we always use their input and feedback from time to time to improve human errors, if any, that may occur during the publishing processes involved. We invite you to participate in our errata submission process to ensure our books remain accurate and up to date. Please help us reach out to readers who might have difficulties due to unforeseen errors. Please write to us at ***errata@arcchieonline.com***.

When submitting errata, please include the following information:
Book Title
Reference#
Author(s)
Page Number
Description of the Error
Suggested Correction (if applicable)

The **ARCCHIE Publications** Family highly appreciates your support, suggestions, and feedback.

Sharing Your Perspective and Providing Feedback

Your perspective is invaluable to us, as it helps us enhance our content and gather your feedback. We warmly welcome all forms of feedback. Please feel free to send us an email at **feedback@arcchieonline.com**, mentioning the book title in the subject line of your message.

Book Review Invitation

We kindly invite you to share your thoughts. After you've read and engaged with this book, consider leaving a review on the platform where you acquired it. Your impartial feedback can greatly assist potential readers in making informed decisions. Your reviews provide valuable insights for us at **Arcchie**, helping us better understand your perspectives on our products, and they offer authors the chance to appreciate your feedback on their work.

Piracy

Should you encounter unauthorized reproductions of our publications in any digital format on the internet, we kindly request your assistance in pinpointing their locations or website sources. Please reach out to us at **copyright@arcchieonline.com** and include a link to the infringing material.

If you possess expertise in a particular subject and wish to participate in the creation or contribution to a book, please visit ***authors.arcchieonline.com***. We welcome you and assist you to start your authorship journey with **ARCCHIE PUBLICATIONS**.

TABLE OF CONTENTS

Chapter 1

Introduction to Databases

Databases are the foundation for nearly every modern digital system—from banking apps and e-commerce platforms to healthcare systems and social media networks. They enable organizations to store, organize, access, and manage vast amounts of data with precision and efficiency. At the heart of managing these structured data systems lies Structured Query Language (SQL)—the universal language used to communicate with relational databases.

In this chapter, we'll begin by exploring the core principles behind databases: what they are, why they matter, and how they function in real-world scenarios. You'll learn about the different types of databases, focusing on relational databases, which remain the most widely used model in academia and industry. We'll then delve into how SQL empowers users—from data analysts to software developers—to create, manipulate, and query data effectively.

Whether you're preparing for academic research, a data-driven role in the tech industry, or simply aiming to build a solid foundation in data management, this chapter will set the stage for your journey into the world of SQL and relational databases.

We will cover the following topics:
- What is a Database?
- Types of Databases: Relational vs. Non-Relational
- Introduction to Database Management Systems (DBMS)
- Overview of SQL and Its Applications
- Understanding Tables, Columns, Rows, and Keys

What is Database?

A database is a structured and systematic collection of data designed for efficient access, management, and updating. Rather than keeping information in scattered files or spreadsheets, databases bring organization and consistency to data storage and retrieval. They serve as the backbone for a wide range of applications across industries, from small businesses tracking inventory to global enterprises managing millions of customer records.

In academic terms, a database is more than just a storage container—it's a digital infrastructure that supports data integrity, retrieval, manipulation, and security. It provides a centralized environment where information can be shared, queried, and modified with precision and control.

In the real world, databases are everywhere. For instance, when you make an online purchase, your transaction details are recorded in a retailer's database. Hospitals use databases to store patient histories, while universities manage student records, course registrations, and academic transcripts through them.

One of the most widely used types of database is the relational database. These systems organize data into tables, each consisting of rows (records) and columns (fields or attributes). This tabular format makes it easy to establish relationships between different data sets and perform complex queries efficiently. Relational databases offer robust support for scalability, data consistency, and concurrent user access, making them a preferred choice for applications that require high reliability and performance.

Types of Databases

Understanding the different types of databases is foundational to mastering database management systems. Broadly speaking, databases fall into two main categories: Relational and Non-Relational. Each type has distinct characteristics and use cases, and choosing the right one depends on the data's structure and the application's nature.

Relational Databases (RDBMS)

Relational databases are the most traditional and widely used type of database. They organize data into tables, also known as relations, each consisting of rows and columns. Each row represents a single record, and each column holds a specific attribute of that record. One of the key strengths of RDBMS is the ability to define and enforce relationships between different tables using keys—typically primary and foreign keys.

These databases follow **Structured Query Language** (**SQL**) standards to insert, retrieve, update, and delete data, ensuring consistency and reliability through a set of rules known as **ACID** properties (Atomicity, Consistency, Isolation, Durability).

Relational databases are ideal for applications where data integrity and complex queries are essential, such as banking systems, inventory management, or academic institutions.

The following are the popular **RDBMS**

- Microsoft SQL Server - Widely used in enterprise environments for large-scale, mission-critical applications.
- MySQL - An open-source RDBMS known for its speed and ease of use, especially popular in web applications.
- PostgreSQL - A powerful, open-source RDBMS with advanced features and standards compliance, suitable for both simple and complex projects.
- Oracle Database - A robust, enterprise-grade RDBMS with strong performance, scalability, and security features.

Non-Relational Databases (NoSQL)

Non-relational databases, often called **NoSQL** databases, are designed to handle unstructured, semi-structured, or rapidly changing data that doesn't fit neatly into tables. Unlike **RDBMS**, they do not rely on fixed schemas or **SQL** for interactions. Instead, they offer flexible data models, which makes them particularly effective for handling big data, real-time analytics, and distributed systems.

NoSQL databases are optimized for performance, scalability, and availability—often sacrificing some aspects of consistency for speed and horizontal scaling. They're commonly used in applications such as social media platforms, IoT systems, content management, and recommendation engines

Common types of **NoSQL** databases include:

- Document-oriented (e.g., **MongoDB**) - Store data as JSON-like documents, making them easy for developers to work with.
- Column-family stores (e.g., **Cassandra**) - Efficient for handling large volumes of data spread across many machines.
- Key-value stores (e.g., **Redis**) - Extremely fast, lightweight databases ideal for caching and session storage.

Each system supports different use cases and data models, allowing developers to choose the best fit based on application requirements.

Introduction to SQL

Structured Query Language, more commonly known as **SQL** (pronounced "ess-cue-ell" or "sequel"), is the standard language used to communicate with relational databases. Whether managing an extensive corporate database or querying a small academic dataset, **SQL** provides a consistent, powerful way to store, retrieve, update, and delete data. Its efficiency and versatility make it an indispensable skill for anyone working with data.

SQL is widely used across industries—from finance and healthcare to retail and tech—by professionals such as data analysts, software developers, business intelligence specialists, and database administrators. Its relevance extends beyond computer science; researchers, engineers, and even marketing professionals increasingly rely on **SQL** to extract meaningful insights from structured data.

Learning **SQL** is a foundational step for students pursuing careers in data-driven fields. With **SQL**, you gain direct control over data stored in relational databases, enabling you to ask precise questions and generate customized reports that support data-informed decision-making.

Understanding Tables, Columns, Rows, and Keys

At the core of any relational database is a table—a structured format for storing data in a logical and accessible way. To truly understand how **SQL** works, it's important to grasp the building blocks of these tables:

- Columns: each column represents a specific attribute or field within the table. For example, in a table tracking product sales, columns might include **ProductName, SaleDate**, **QuantitySold**, and **Price**. Every column is defined by a data type (such as **integer**, **text**, or **date**), which dictates what information it can hold.
- Rows a row is a single record or entry in the table. Each row contains data for all the defined columns. Consider a row as a real-world transaction—one sale of a particular product on a specific date, for example.
- A Primary Key is a column—or a combination of columns—uniquely identifying each table row. No two rows can share the same primary key value, which ensures data integrity by preventing duplicate entries. For example, a **CustomerID** or **InvoiceNumber** can serve as a primary key.
- Foreign Key: a foreign key is used to create a relationship between two tables. It refers to the primary Key in another table and is a bridge between them. For example, in a database with a **Customers** table and an **Orders** table, the **CustomerID** in the **Orders** table would be a foreign key referencing the **CustomerID** in the **Customers** table. This allows related data to be stored efficiently without redundancy.

Creating the GlobalMart Database

We need a structured database to practice before working with SQL queries and data operations.

Why GlobalMart Database?

GlobalMart represents a mid-sized retail business that sells a variety of products across multiple locations. It operates online and through physical stores, handling diverse inventory, customer transactions, supplier relationships, and employee records. Using **GlobalMart** as our case study, we can explore real-world database concepts that businesses use daily—such as inventory management, sales tracking, customer relationships, and supply chain operations.

Setting Up the Database

We will create a structured database to serve as the foundation for our learning exercises. In SQL, a database is a logically organized collection of data that enables efficient storage, retrieval, and management of information. To create the **GlobalMart** database and tables, we use the following **SQL** command (**Chapter 2** will demonstrate these **SQL** commands in more detail):

```
-- Create the GlobalMart database
CREATE DATABASE GlobalMart;

-- Switch to the GlobalMart database
USE GlobalMart;

-- Create a table for storing sales data
CREATE TABLE Sales (
   SaleID INT PRIMARY KEY IDENTITY(1,1),
   ProductName NVARCHAR(100),
   QuantitySold INT,
   SaleDate DATE,
   Revenue DECIMAL(10, 2)
);

-- Create a table for storing purchase data
CREATE TABLE Purchases (
   PurchaseID INT PRIMARY KEY IDENTITY(1,1),
   SupplierName NVARCHAR(100),
   ProductName NVARCHAR(100),
   QuantityPurchased INT,
   PurchaseDate DATE,
   Cost DECIMAL(10, 2)
);.
```

Summary

In this chapter, we laid the foundation for understanding databases and highlighted the essential role of SQL in data management. We began by examining the fundamental principles of databases before progressing to the practical implementation of a basic database for GlobalMart. Through this process, we designed and structured tables to manage sales and purchase transactions, reinforcing how data is stored and organized within a relational database system.

Building on this groundwork, the next chapter will delve into retrieving data efficiently using **SQL** queries. We will explore key retrieval techniques, including **SELECT** statements, filtering data with **WHERE** clauses, sorting results, and leveraging built-in **SQL** functions to extract meaningful insights. By the end of the next chapter, you will have the skills to query databases effectively and transform raw data into valuable information.

Chapter 2
Getting Started with SQL

In the previous chapter, we explored the foundational concepts of databases. We introduced **SQL** (**Structured Query Language**) as the standard language for managing and manipulating relational data. Building on that understanding, this chapter guides you through the practical steps of getting started with **SQL**. You'll learn how to set up your **SQL** environment, become familiar with essential commands, and begin executing queries to retrieve, insert, update, and manage data within a database system. By the end of this chapter, you will have hands-on experience with **SQL** basics—laying the groundwork for more advanced database operations in the chapters ahead.

In this chapter, we will cover:

- Installing and Setting Up Microsoft SQL Server
- Overview of SQL Server Management Studio (**SSMS**)
- Essential SQL Commands: **CREATE, INSERT, SELECT, UPDATE, DELETE**
- Writing and Executing Queries

Overview of SQL Server Management Studio (SSMS)

Understanding how to interact with a database system is foundational for anyone studying data management or working with structured data. In this section, we'll introduce SQL Server Management Studio (**SSMS**)—a powerful, user-friendly environment for managing SQL Server databases. Whether you're a novice or brushing up on database fundamentals, SSMS provides the tools to create, modify, and query databases through graphical interfaces and direct SQL commands.

SQL Server Management Studio (**SSMS**) is an integrated environment developed by Microsoft that enables users to manage SQL Server infrastructure. Designed to simplify database administration, SSMS provides beginners and professionals access to a range of tools and functionalities. Some of the key components include:

- Object Explorer: This tool acts like a control center, listing all server objects—such as databases, tables, views, and stored procedures—in a hierarchical tree view. This allows users to easily navigate and manage various elements of the database.
- Query Editor: A dedicated workspace for writing and executing SQL queries. It

supports syntax highlighting, code formatting, and script execution, making query development intuitive and efficient.

- Results Pane: This pane displays the output of executed queries in tabular format, helping users interpret the results immediately and verify the correctness of their SQL statements.

Working with SQL: Basic Commands

Structured Query Language (**SQL**) is the standard language for interacting with relational databases. In this section, we'll walk through the basic commands to create a database, define tables, insert data, retrieve records, update existing values, and delete entries.

Create Database

To begin with, we'll create a new database called **GlobalMart**, which will store sales and purchase-related information for a fictional retail company.

```
-- Create a new database
CREATE DATABASE GlobalMart;

-- Switch to the GlobalMart database
USE GlobalMart;
```

Note: The **CREATE DATABASE** statement initializes a new database, while the **USE** command sets it as the current working database.

Creating Tables

Now that we have a database, we need to define the structure of the data we plan to store. This involves creating tables for different data categories. Let's create two tables: one for sales and another for purchases.

```
-- Create a table for sales data
CREATE TABLE Sales (
   SaleID INT PRIMARY KEY IDENTITY(1,1),
   ProductName NVARCHAR(100),
   QuantitySold INT,
   SaleDate DATE,
   Revenue DECIMAL(10, 2)
);
```

- **SaleID** is the unique identifier for each record and is set to auto-increment.
- **ProductName** stores the name of the product sold.
- **QuantitySold** represents the number of items sold.
- **SaleDate** is the date of the transaction.
- **Revenue** captures the monetary value of the sale.

```
-- Create a table for purchase data
CREATE TABLE Purchases (
   PurchaseID INT PRIMARY KEY IDENTITY(1,1),
   SupplierName NVARCHAR(100),
   ProductName NVARCHAR(100),
   QuantityPurchased INT,
   PurchaseDate DATE,
   Cost DECIMAL(10, 2)
);
```

Here, Purchases hold information about inventory procurement from suppliers.

Inserting Data

Once the tables are created, we can populate them with sample data using the **INSERT INTO** command.

```
-- Insert data into the Sales table
INSERT INTO Sales (ProductName, QuantitySold, SaleDate, Revenue)
VALUES ('Laptop', 5, '2024-02-01', 5000.00),
     ('Smartphone', 10, '2024-02-02', 7000.00);

-- Insert data into the Purchases table
INSERT INTO Purchases (SupplierName, ProductName, QuantityPurchased,
PurchaseDate, Cost)
VALUES ('ABC Suppliers', 'Laptop', 10, '2024-01-25', 8000.00),
     ('XYZ Electronics', 'Smartphone', 15, '2024-01-26', 9000.00);
```

These statements insert initial records into our tables, simulating a small but meaningful dataset for learning and experimentation.

Retrieving Data

The **SELECT** statement is one of the most frequently used commands in **SQL**. It allows us to view the contents of a table.

```
-- Retrieve all data from the Sales table
SELECT * FROM Sales;
```

```
-- Retrieve all data from the Purchases table
SELECT * FROM Purchases;
```

The asterisk (*) tells **SQL** to fetch all columns for every row in the specified table.

Updating Data

Sometimes, data needs to be corrected or updated. The **UPDATE** statement allows you to modify existing records based on specific conditions.

```
-- Update Revenue for a specific sale
UPDATE Sales
SET Revenue = 5500.00
WHERE SaleID = 1;
```

This command updates the Revenue value of the sale with **SaleID** = 1.

Always use a **WHERE** clause with **UPDATE** to avoid unintentionally changing all records.

Deleting Data

When records are no longer needed or were entered incorrectly, they can be removed using the **DELETE** statement.

```
-- Delete a specific sale record
DELETE FROM Sales
WHERE SaleID = 2;
```

This statement removes the sale record where the SaleID equals 2.

Like **UPDATE**, using **DELETE** without a **WHERE** clause will remove all records from the table.

Summary

This chapter explored the SQL Server Management Studio (**SSMS**) environment. We learned how to interact with SQL Server databases using basic SQL commands. Specifically, we covered how to:

- Create a new database and switch to it
- Define tables for storing structured data
- Insert, retrieve, update, and delete data using core **SQL** statements

These operations lay the groundwork for more advanced querying and database design techniques that we will explore in subsequent chapters.

In the next chapter, we'll delve into more advanced **SQL** operations, including filtering results using conditions, applying sorting and aggregation, and retrieving specific subsets of data using clauses like **WHERE**, **ORDER BY**, and **GROUP BY**.

Let's continue building your confidence in writing precise, efficient, and powerful **SQL** queries.

Chapter 3

Data Retrieval Techniques

In the previous chapter, we laid the foundation for working with SQL by learning how to create tables, insert records, and retrieve data using fundamental queries. These basic commands are essential for any database interaction. Still, as you progress in your learning—and eventually in your career—you'll find that real-world data retrieval often demands more nuanced and powerful techniques.

In this chapter, we focus on advanced data retrieval methods that will allow you to write more efficient, flexible, and insightful queries. Mastering these concepts not only helps streamline your **SQL** operations but also enables you to extract meaningful patterns and summaries from complex datasets—skills that are highly valued in academic research, business analytics, and data-driven decision-making.

We will explore the following key techniques:

- Using the **DISTINCT** Clause to Eliminate Duplicate Results
- Applying Column Aliases for Improved Readability
- Filtering Data Using the **WHERE Clause** and **Logical Operators**
- Sorting Results with the **ORDER BY** Clause
- Utilizing Aggregate Functions (**SUM, AVG, COUNT, MIN, MAX**)
- Grouping Data with **GROUP BY** and Filtering Groups with **HAVING**

Removing Duplicates with DISTINCT

In many real-world datasets, duplicate values are shared. SQL provides the **DISTINCT** keyword to ensure that your queries return only unique entries. This clause eliminates duplicate records from the result set, helping you avoid redundancy and focus on distinctive values.

```
-- Retrieve unique product names from the Sales table
SELECT DISTINCT ProductName
FROM Sales;
```

In this example, if the Sales table contains multiple entries for the same product, only one instance of each product name will appear in the output. This is especially useful when generating lists for drop-down menus, summaries, or reports where repetition is not meaningful.

Using Column Aliases

Column aliases are used to rename columns in a query's output, making results easier to interpret—particularly in reports or visualizations. An alias acts as a temporary label that improves the readability of the result set without altering the underlying table schema.

```
-- Assigning an alias to columns for clearer output
SELECT ProductName AS 'Item', Revenue AS 'Total Revenue'
FROM Sales;
```

ProductName is displayed as Item, and Revenue is labeled Total Revenue. Aliases are especially useful when working with expressions or aggregate functions or when you want the output to match business-friendly terminology.

Filtering Data Using the **WHERE** Clause

```
-- Retrieve sales data for the product 'Laptop' only
SELECT *
FROM Sales
WHERE ProductName = 'Laptop';
```

This query filters the dataset to return only those records where the ProductName is Laptop, excluding all other products. This type of filtering is crucial when analyzing subsets of data for business decisions or research.

Using Logical Operators (**AND**, **OR**, **NOT**)
Logical operators help combine multiple conditions in a WHERE clause, offering greater flexibility in data filtering.

```
-- Retrieve sales data for both 'Laptop' and 'Smartphone'
SELECT *
FROM Sales
WHERE ProductName = 'Laptop' OR ProductName = 'Smartphone';
```

In this query:

- **OR** ensures that records matching either product are included.
- You can also use **AND** to require that all conditions be actual or **NOT** to exclude specific matches.

These logical tools allow you to build complex queries tailored to real-world requirements.

Sorting Data Using **ORDER BY**

The **ORDER BY** clause sorts the result set based on one or more columns. By default, the sorting is in ascending order (**ASC**), but you can explicitly specify descending order (**DESC**) if needed.

```
-- Retrieve all sales, sorted by Revenue in descending order
SELECT *
FROM Sales
ORDER BY Revenue DESC;
```

Sorting data is critical in identifying top-performing products, ranking customers, or preparing data for presentation.

Using Aggregate Function

Aggregate functions perform calculations across multiple rows, providing summary-level insights from large datasets. Common aggregate functions include **SUM()**, **AVG()**, **MAX()**, **MIN()**, and **COUNT()**.

```
-- Calculate total Revenue from all sales
SELECT SUM(Revenue) AS TotalRevenue
FROM Sales;
```

This query returns the combined Revenue from all transactions. Aggregate functions are widely used in financial reports, dashboards, and performance metrics.

Grouping Data with **GROUP** BY and Filtering with **HAVING**

The **GROUP BY** clause aggregates data based on one or more columns, allowing you to perform operations like totals or averages within each group. The **HAVING** clause then filters the grouped results like **WHERE** filters individual rows.

```
-- Find total Revenue per product
SELECT ProductName, SUM(Revenue) AS TotalRevenue
FROM Sales
GROUP BY ProductName;
```

This query groups the sales data by product and calculates the total Revenue for each product.

```
-- Retrieve products with total Revenue greater than $5000
SELECT ProductName, SUM(Revenue) AS TotalRevenue
```

```
FROM Sales
GROUP BY ProductName
HAVING SUM(Revenue) > 5000;
```

Here, the **HAVING** clause filters out products whose total Revenue is **$5,000** or less. This approach is beneficial for identifying high-performing items or outliers in your data.

Summary

This chapter explored essential **SQL techniques** for refining and interpreting your data. From removing duplicates using **DISTINCT** to filtering with **WHERE**, summarizing with aggregate functions, and organizing your results using **ORDER BY** and **GROUP BY**, these tools form the backbone of advanced data retrieval.

By mastering these concepts, you'll be equipped to extract meaningful, actionable insights from even the largest and most complex datasets—a vital skill for data analysts, developers, and database administrators alike.

In the next chapter, we'll build on this foundation by exploring **SQL Joins**, which allow you to combine data from multiple related tables. Understanding joins is key to performing powerful multi-table queries and constructing relational insights.

Chapter 4

SQL Joins – Combining Data from Multiple Tables

In the previous chapter, we learned how to retrieve and manipulate data using filters, sorting options, and aggregate functions. While those techniques are essential for working with individual tables, real-world data is rarely confined to a single table. Instead, information is typically spread across multiple related tables to ensure data integrity, minimize redundancy, and support efficient storage.

To extract meaningful insights from such structured data, we must learn how to combine—or "**join**"—tables effectively. This chapter introduces the concept of SQL Joins, a fundamental mechanism that allows us to query related data across multiple tables and build rich, multi-dimensional result sets.

By the end of this chapter, you will be able to:

- Understand how tables relate to each other in a relational database.
- Identify and use different types of **SQL** joins: **INNER JOIN**, **LEFT JOIN**, RIGHT **JOIN** and **FULL OUTER JOIN**.
- Write join queries to fetch relevant data from multiple tables.
- Apply joins to real-world business scenarios.

Understanding Database Relationships

Relational databases organize information into separate tables, each focusing on a specific subject or entity, such as customers, products, or orders. These tables are linked together using keys—specifically, primary keys (which uniquely identify each record in a table) and foreign keys (which create connections between tables).

Real-World Analogy: TechRetail Corp

Let's consider a fictional company, **TechRetail Corp**, which sells electronic products. The company's database is designed with the following tables:

- **Customers** - Contains customer information (e.g., **name** and **contact**).

- **Products** – Store details of each product available for sale.
- **Orders** – Tracks purchases, linking each order to a customer and a product.

This structure reflects a normalized design that avoids duplication and makes the data more manageable.

Creating the Sample Tables

Here's how these tables might be created in **SQL**:

```
-- Customers Table
CREATE TABLE Customers (
   CustomerID INT PRIMARY KEY,
   CustomerName VARCHAR(100),
   ContactEmail VARCHAR(100)
);

-- Products Table
CREATE TABLE Products (
   ProductID INT PRIMARY KEY,
   ProductName VARCHAR(100),
   Price DECIMAL(10,2)
);

-- Orders Table
CREATE TABLE Orders (
   OrderID INT PRIMARY KEY,
   CustomerID INT,
   ProductID INT,
   OrderDate DATE,
   Quantity INT,
   TotalAmount DECIMAL(10,2),
   FOREIGN KEY (CustomerID) REFERENCES Customers(CustomerID),
   FOREIGN KEY (ProductID) REFERENCES Products(ProductID)
);
```

Notice how the **Orders** table references the **Customers** and Products tables using foreign keys. This allows us to relate an order to the customer who placed it and the purchased product.

INNER JOIN – Fetching Matching Records

The **INNER JOIN** is the most commonly used join in **SQL**. It returns only those records with a match between the joined tables. If a row in either table does not have a corresponding match in the other, it is excluded from the result set.

```
-- Get All Orders with Customer and Product Details
SELECT
   Customers.CustomerName,
   Orders.OrderID,
   Products.ProductName,
   Orders.Quantity,
   Orders.TotalAmount
FROM Orders
INNER JOIN Customers ON Orders.CustomerID = Customers.CustomerID
INNER JOIN Products ON Orders.ProductID = Products.ProductID;
```

Explanation: This query retrieves customer names, order details, and product information—but only for records where matching entries exist in all three tables.

LEFT JOIN - Include All Records from the Left Table

A **LEFT JOIN** returns all records from the left table (the one listed first) and the matched records from the right table. **NULL** values are shown for the right table's columns if no match exists.

```
-- List All Customers and Their Orders (If Any)
SELECT
   Customers.CustomerName,
   Orders.OrderID,
   Orders.OrderDate,
   Orders.TotalAmount
FROM Customers
LEFT JOIN Orders ON Customers.CustomerID = Orders.CustomerID;
```

RIGHT JOIN - Include All Records from the Right Table

A **RIGHT JOIN** works similarly to a **LEFT JOIN**, but in reverse. It returns all records from the right table and matching rows from the left table. **NULLs** are returned for the left table's columns where no match exists.

```
-- Show All Orders, Even If Customer Info Is Missing
SELECT
   Orders.OrderID,
   Customers.CustomerName,
   Orders.TotalAmount
FROM Orders
```

```
RIGHT JOIN Customers ON Orders.CustomerID = Customers.CustomerID;
```

Explanation: This scenario might occur if, for example, some customer data was accidentally deleted while order records remained. The query ensures that no orders are lost from the report.

FULL OUTER JOIN - Combine All Records

A **FULL OUTER JOIN** returns all records from both tables. The result will show the matched data if there is a match between the two tables. Where no match exists, **NULL** values fill in the gaps for the missing side.

```
-- Display All Customers and All Orders, Matched or Not
SELECT
   Customers.CustomerName,
   Orders.OrderID,
   Orders.TotalAmount
FROM Customers
FULL OUTER JOIN Orders ON Customers.CustomerID = Orders.CustomerID;
```

Explanation: This type of join is helpful for comprehensive reporting—especially when you want to ensure that no data is excluded, even if the records aren't perfectly matched.

Real-World Relevance of Joins

- E-commerce platforms use joins to combine customer, order, and product data for analytics and reporting.
- Healthcare systems join patient records with appointment schedules and test results.
- Educational institutions link students, courses, and grades to generate performance reports.

Understanding joins equips you to work with relational databases in virtually any industry, making this a critical skill for aspiring data professionals, analysts, and developers.

Summary

This chapter explored how **SQL** Joins enable us to combine data from multiple tables, a core concept in working with relational databases.

We learned how to use:

- **INNER JOIN** to retrieve matching records from related tables.
- **LEFT JOIN** and **RIGHT JOIN** will include unmatched data from one side.
- **FULL OUTER JOIN** is to return all data from both tables, whether matched or not.

We also saw practical examples of how joins help model real-world business scenarios, like customer purchases and product tracking.

In the next chapter, we'll explore Subqueries and Nested **Queries**—advanced techniques that allow us to write more powerful and dynamic **SQL** statements by embedding one query within another. These tools help handle complex business questions and optimize database queries.

Chapter 5
Subqueries and Nested Queries

In the previous chapter, we explored SQL Joins, which allow us to retrieve and combine data from multiple tables using shared columns. While joins are essential for relational data analysis, they are insufficient when dealing with more advanced or hierarchical queries. Often, we need to perform a query within another query—for example, when filtering results based on the outcome of another operation. This is where subqueries, also known as nested queries, become highly valuable.

In this chapter, we will delve into:

- What subqueries and how they work
- Types of subqueries: **Single-row**, **Multi-row**, and **Correlated**
- Using subqueries within the context of **SELECT**, **INSERT**, **UPDATE**, and **DELETE** statements
- Real-world use cases to strengthen your understanding

Understanding Subqueries

A subquery is a **SQL** query embedded inside another query. It is executed first, and its result is then passed to the outer (main) query for further processing. Subqueries enable stepwise logic in **SQL** and help decompose complex problems into manageable parts.

You can place subqueries in several clauses, such as **WHERE**, **FROM**, or **SELECT**. Depending on where they are used and how they interact with the outer query, subqueries are categorized as single-row, multi-row, or correlated subqueries.

Use Case: TechRetail Corp

Let's continue with our fictional company, **TechRetail Corp**, which wants to analyze its operations—sales, purchases, and production data—over the past five years. Throughout this chapter, we'll use sample data from TechRetail's database to illustrate the use of subqueries.

```
-- Create a Sales table
CREATE TABLE Sales (
  SaleID INT PRIMARY KEY,
  CustomerID INT,
  ProductID INT,
  SaleDate DATE,
  QuantitySold INT,
  TotalAmount DECIMAL(10,2)
);

-- Create a Product table
CREATE TABLE Products (
  ProductID INT PRIMARY KEY,
  ProductName VARCHAR(100),
  Price DECIMAL(10,2)
);
```

These two tables form the basis of our examples: **Sales** holds transaction data, while **Products** stores product information.

Single-Row Subqueries

A single-row subquery returns exactly one value (one row with one column). These are typically used with comparison operators such as **=, <, >, <=, or >=.**

```
-- Find the Most Expensive Product
SELECT ProductName, Price
FROM Products
WHERE Price = (SELECT MAX(Price) FROM Products);
```

Explanation: The subquery (**SELECT MAX(Price) FROM Products**) returns the highest price from the Products table. The outer query selects the product(s) that match this price. Since **MAX()** returns a single value, the subquery is considered a single-row subquery.

Multi-Row Subqueries

A multi-row subquery returns multiple values. These are used with operators like **IN**, **ANY**, or **ALL** to compare a value against a results list.

```
SELECT ProductName
FROM Products
WHERE ProductID IN (
  SELECT ProductID
  FROM Sales
```

```
  WHERE QuantitySold > 1
);
```

Explanation: The subquery retrieves all **ProductIDs** from the **Sales** table where the quantity sold exceeds one. The outer query then fetches the corresponding product names from the **Products** table.

Correlated Subqueries

A correlated subquery references a column from the outer query and is evaluated repeatedly—once for each row processed by the outer query. These are more advanced and powerful, especially when working with row-level comparisons.

```
-- Find Customers Who Spend Above Their Own Average
SELECT CustomerID, TotalAmount
FROM Sales S1
WHERE TotalAmount > (
  SELECT AVG(TotalAmount)
  FROM Sales S2
  WHERE S1.CustomerID = S2.CustomerID
);
```

Explanation: For each row in **Sales** (aliased as **S1**), the subquery calculates the customer's average transaction amount from the same **Sales** table (aliased as **S2**). The outer query then filters for purchases higher than the customer's average. This type of subquery is tightly coupled with the outer query and requires row-by-row evaluation.

Subqueries with INSERT, UPDATE, and DELETE

Subqueries are not limited to **SELECT** statements—they also play a critical role in **INSERT**, **UPDATE**, and **DELETE** operations, making data manipulation more intelligent and conditional.

```
-- Add High-Value Customers
INSERT INTO HighValueCustomers (CustomerID, TotalSpent)
SELECT CustomerID, SUM(TotalAmount)
FROM Sales
GROUP BY CustomerID
HAVING SUM(TotalAmount) > 5000;
```

Explanation: This subquery aggregates total spending per customer and filters those exceeding **$5,000**. These qualifying customers are inserted into the **HighValueCustomers** table.

```
-- Increase Prices for High-Selling Products
UPDATE Products
SET Price = Price * 1.1
WHERE ProductID IN (
  SELECT DISTINCT ProductID
  FROM Sales
  WHERE TotalAmount > 1000
);
```

Explanation: This updates the price of products that appear in high-value sales (above **$1,000**). The **DISTINCT** keyword ensures each product is only updated once, even if it appears in multiple sales records.

```
-- Remove Unsold Products
DELETE FROM Products
WHERE ProductID NOT IN (
  SELECT DISTINCT ProductID
  FROM Sales
);
```

Explanation: This deletes products that have never been sold. The subquery identifies all **ProductIDs** that appear in the **Sales** table, and the outer query removes any products not on that list.

Summary

Subqueries are powerful SQL tools that allow you to write modular, layered queries for complex data operations. They enable filtering, conditional logic, and dynamic comparisons, all within a single SQL statement.

In this chapter, we examined:

- The concept and structure of subqueries
- Differences between single-row, multi-row, and correlated subqueries
- Practical examples using **SELECT**, **INSERT**, **UPDATE**, and **DELETE** operations
- As you continue to build your SQL skillset, mastering subqueries will allow you to think more analytically and work more effectively with real-world datasets.

In the next chapter, we will explore Aggregate Functions and **Grouping Data**. In this section, you will learn how to summarize large volumes of data using functions like **SUM()**, **AVG()**, and **COUNT()** in combination with **GROUP BY**.

Chapter 6

Views and Stored Procedures

In the previous chapter, we explored subqueries and how they enable more efficient data retrieval from complex database structures. Building on that foundation, this chapter introduces two powerful SQL features: Views and Stored Procedures. These constructs are essential for optimizing queries, organizing database logic, and enhancing performance and security in real-world applications.

By the end of this chapter, you'll have a strong grasp of:

- What Views are and how they function
- How to create, manage, and modify Views
- The advantages Views bring to database design
- An introduction to Stored Procedures and their role in SQL
- How to create and execute Stored Procedures
- Working with parameters and return values in Stored Procedures

What Are Views?

A View is a virtual table in SQL. It doesn't store data physically but instead provides a window into one or more underlying tables based on a defined query. Every time a View is accessed, the database runs the query that defines it and returns the resulting dataset.

Views are beneficial for:

- Simplifying access to complex joins or calculated fields
- Restricting user access to sensitive data
- Creating customized data presentations without altering the underlying tables

Think of a View as a "**read-only lens**" through which you can examine selected parts of a database.

Creating and Managing Views

Let's look at how to create a simple View.

Example: Create a View for high-value orders (total amount greater than **$5000**):

```
CREATE VIEW HighValueOrders AS
SELECT OrderID, CustomerID, TotalAmount
FROM Orders
WHERE TotalAmount > 5000;
```

This View does not store data. Instead, it dynamically pulls the relevant information from the **Orders** table each time it's queried.

Using Views

Once created, a View can be used like a regular table in your queries.

```
SELECT * FROM HighValueOrders;
```

This query fetches all columns defined in the **HighValueOrders** View. It simplifies access to filtered data without requiring the original filter logic every time.

Updating a View

You can modify the definition of an existing View using the **ALTER VIEW** statement. However, keep in mind that not all Views are updatable. Typically, Views based on a single table, without aggregate functions or complex joins, are updatable.

Example: Add **OrderDate** to the View:

```
ALTER VIEW HighValueOrders AS
SELECT OrderID, CustomerID, TotalAmount, OrderDate
FROM Orders
WHERE TotalAmount > 5000;
```

Dropping a View

To permanently remove a View from the database:

```
DROP VIEW HighValueOrders;
```

Advantages of Using Views

- Simplifies complex **SQL**: Developers and users can access a simplified data version

without writing lengthy queries.
- Enhances data **security**: Views can expose only the necessary columns, shielding sensitive fields like passwords or salaries.
- Improves **maintainability**: If the underlying table structure changes, the View can remain unchanged, providing a stable interface.
- Provides **abstraction**: Views abstract database complexity from end-users and applications.

Introduction to Stored Procedures

A Stored Procedure is a precompiled collection of one or more **SQL** statements that are stored on the database server and can be executed repeatedly.

Stored procedures are invaluable when:
- Performing repetitive operations (e.g., generating monthly reports)
- Applying business logic directly within the database
- Enhancing performance by reducing network traffic and query parsing time

Creating a Stored Procedure

Example: Retrieve all orders for a specific customer:

```
CREATE PROCEDURE GetCustomerOrders
  @CustomerID INT
AS
BEGIN
  SELECT OrderID, OrderDate, TotalAmount
  FROM Orders
  WHERE CustomerID = @CustomerID;
END;
```

This procedure takes a **CustomerID** as input and returns the list of orders for that customer.

Executing a Stored Procedure

Stored procedures are executed using the **EXEC** (or **EXECUTE**) command.

```
EXEC GetCustomerOrders @CustomerID = 101;
```

This command runs the procedure and returns the relevant order data for customer **101**.

Stored Procedures with **Output Parameters**

Stored procedures can also return values using output parameters. This is especially helpful when you must compute and return a single result, such as a total or average.

Example: Calculate the total **sales** for a **customer**:

```
CREATE PROCEDURE GetTotalSales
  @CustomerID INT,
  @TotalSales DECIMAL(10,2) OUTPUT
AS
BEGIN
  SELECT @TotalSales = SUM(TotalAmount)
  FROM Orders
  WHERE CustomerID = @CustomerID;
END;
```

To call this procedure and capture the output:

```
DECLARE @TotalSales DECIMAL(10,2);
EXEC GetTotalSales @CustomerID = 101, @TotalSales = @TotalSales OUTPUT;
PRINT @TotalSales;
```

Summary

In this chapter, we explored two fundamental SQL tools—views and Stored Procedures—that help streamline, organize, and secure database operations.

- Views act as virtual tables derived from SQL queries. They simplify access to complex data, enforce access control, and provide consistent data representations.
- Stored Procedures encapsulate reusable SQL logic, automate repetitive tasks, and support dynamic operations through input and output parameters.

In the next chapter, we will explore Indexes and Performance Optimization, examining how to speed up query execution and ensure databases scale efficiently.

Chapter 7

Transactions and Concurrency Control

In the previous chapter, we examined Indexes and Performance Optimization, crucial tools for accelerating query execution and enhancing overall database efficiency. Now, we focus on another foundational concept in database management: Transactions and Concurrency Control. These concepts are essential for ensuring that database operations remain reliable, consistent, and error-free—especially in environments where multiple users access or manipulate data simultaneously.

This chapter will help you:

- Understand what transactions are and why they are important
- Explore the **ACID** properties that govern transaction behavior
- Learn how to implement transactions using **SQL**
- Identify common concurrency issues and how to handle them
- Study **SQL** isolation levels and their implications
- Discover locking mechanisms used to manage concurrent access

Mastering these principles is key to maintaining data integrity and preventing conflicts, whether working on a multi-user database or designing enterprise-level applications.

Understanding Transactions

A transaction in **SQL** is a logical work unit consisting of one or more **SQL** statements executed as a single operation. These statements are grouped together so that either all of them succeed—or none of them take effect. This "all-or-nothing" approach ensures consistency and reliability in data operations.

For instance, when transferring funds between two bank accounts, both the withdrawal from one account and the deposit into another must occur together. If one operation fails, the entire transaction should be canceled to maintain the database's correctness.

ACID Properties

Transactions in **SQL** adhere to four essential properties known as **ACID**:

- **Atomicity** ensures that all operations within a transaction are treated as a single unit. If any part of the transaction fails, the entire transaction is rolled back, leaving the database unchanged.
- **Consistency**: Guarantees that a transaction brings the database from one valid state to another, maintaining all predefined rules such as constraints, cascades, and triggers.
- **Isolation**: Ensures that concurrently running transactions do not interfere with each other. Each transaction operates as if it is the only one executing, even when others run in parallel.
- **Durability**: Once a transaction is committed, its changes are permanent—even during a system crash or power failure.

Together, these properties safeguard the integrity and reliability of database systems.

Implementing Transactions in SQL

SQL provides a straightforward mechanism for managing transactions using commands like **BEGIN, COMMIT**, and **ROLLBACK**.

Example: Performing a Transaction Across Multiple Tables

```
BEGIN TRANSACTION;

INSERT INTO Orders (OrderID, CustomerID, OrderDate)
VALUES (101, 501, '2025-03-01');

INSERT INTO OrderDetails (OrderID, ProductID, Quantity)
VALUES (101, 20, 3);

COMMIT TRANSACTION;
```

In this example, the order and its corresponding details are inserted together. If either statement fails, the entire transaction can be rolled back to avoid partial data entry.

Rolling Back a Transaction

Sometimes, an error may occur during the transaction process. To prevent inconsistencies, **SQL** allows you to roll back the entire transaction.

Example: Handling Errors Using **ROLLBACK**

```
BEGIN TRANSACTION;

INSERT INTO Orders (OrderID, CustomerID, OrderDate)
```

```
VALUES (102, 502, '2025-03-02');

-- Simulate an error
IF @@ERROR <> 0
   ROLLBACK TRANSACTION;
ELSE
   COMMIT TRANSACTION;
```

This logic ensures that the transaction is only committed if no errors occur. Otherwise, all changes are undone.

Concurrency Issues in SQL

Concurrency issues may arise when multiple users or applications access the database at the same time. Understanding and handling these issues is crucial for ensuring correct and predictable outcomes.

- **Dirty Read** occurs when a transaction reads data that another transaction has modified but not yet committed. If the other transaction rolls back, the Read becomes invalid.
- **Non-Repeatable Read**: This happens when a transaction reads the same data multiple times and gets different results because another transaction modified the data between reads.
- **Phantom Read**: Arises when a transaction reads a set of rows that match a condition, but new rows satisfying the same condition appear during a subsequent read due to another transaction's insertions.

These issues can lead to inconsistent data if not properly managed.

Isolation Levels

SQL provides several isolation levels to control how transactions interact with each other and manage concurrency. Each level offers a different balance between consistency and performance.

Read Uncommitted

Allows dirty reads. Offers the least isolation and is rarely used in practice.

Read Committed prevents dirty reads by ensuring that only committed data can be read. However, non-repeatable reads are still possible.
Repeatable Read: Prevents both dirty and non-repeatable reads by ensuring that data read once within a transaction cannot change until it ends. Phantom reads, however, may still occur. Serializable strictest level, preventing all concurrency problems. It locks entire data sets, which can reduce performance but ensures maximum consistency.

Example: Setting Serializable Isolation Level

```
SET TRANSACTION ISOLATION LEVEL SERIALIZABLE;

BEGIN TRANSACTION;

SELECT * FROM Orders WHERE CustomerID = 501;

COMMIT TRANSACTION;
```

Choosing the right isolation level depends on the nature of your application and the required balance between accuracy and performance.

Locking Mechanisms

SQL uses locks to manage access to data in concurrent environments. Locks prevent conflicts and maintain data integrity when multiple transactions occur simultaneously.

- **Shared Lock**: This lock allows multiple transactions to read a data item but prevents any from modifying it. It is ideal for read-only operations.
- **Exclusive Lock**: Ensures that only one transaction can read or write to a data item. All others are blocked until the lock is released.

Deadlocks

A deadlock occurs when two or more transactions wait for each other to release locks, causing a standstill. SQL servers like Microsoft SQL Server detect and resolve deadlocks automatically by terminating one of the transactions. Understanding how locks work can help you avoid performance bottlenecks and ensure smooth transaction management.

Summary

This chapter explored the vital role of transactions and concurrency control in **SQL** databases. Key takeaways include:

- Transactions ensure reliable, all-or-nothing data operations.
- The **ACID** properties (**Atomicity, Consistency, Isolation, Durability**) uphold database integrity.
- Concurrency issues such as dirty reads and phantom reads can be mitigated using appropriate isolation levels.
- Locking mechanisms are essential tools for managing access in a multi-user environment.

Mastering these concepts prepares you for real-world applications where data consistency and reliability are non-negotiable. The next chapter will dive into Advanced **SQL** Functions, including powerful analytical and aggregate operations that elevate your data analysis skills.

Chapter 8

Advanced SQL Functions

In the previous chapter, we explored Transactions and Concurrency Control, which are vital for maintaining data integrity in multi-user database environments. These foundational concepts help ensure consistent and reliable database operations even when multiple users access and modify data simultaneously.

Building on that foundation, this chapter focuses on Advanced SQL Functions, which provide robust data analysis, transformation, and summarization tools. These functions are essential for writing expressive and efficient queries—whether you're generating reports, exploring patterns, or preparing datasets for deeper analytics.

By the end of this chapter, you will understand how to harness the full potential of:

- Aggregate Functions
- String Functions
- Date and Time Functions
- Window Functions
- Common Table Expressions (**CTEs**)

Aggregate Functions

Aggregate functions perform calculations across a group of rows and return a single result—ideal for summarizing large datasets. These functions are commonly used with the **GROUP BY** clause to generate statistical insights from tables.

- **SUM()**: Returns the total sum of numeric values.
- **AVG()**: Calculates the average of values in a column.
- **COUNT()**: Counts the number of rows or non-null values.
- **MIN() / MAX()**: Finds a dataset's minimum or maximum value.

Example: Basic Aggregation

```
SELECT
  SUM(TotalAmount) AS TotalSales,
  AVG(TotalAmount) AS AverageSales,
  COUNT(OrderID) AS OrderCount
```

```
FROM Orders;
```

This query provides a quick snapshot of overall sales performance by calculating total sales, average order value, and total number of orders.

String Functions

String functions are designed to manipulate textual data, common in fields like customer names, addresses, and product descriptions. These functions can be used to clean, transform, or extract specific parts of strings.

- **LEN()**: Returns the number of characters in a string.
- **UPPER()** / **LOWER()**: Converts text to uppercase or lowercase.
- **SUBSTRING()**: Extracts a portion of a string based on position.
- **REPLACE()**: Substitutes all instances of a specified substring with another string.

Example: Text Transformation

```
SELECT
  CustomerName,
  UPPER(CustomerName) AS UpperName,
  LOWER(CustomerName) AS LowerName,
  SUBSTRING(CustomerName, 1, 5) AS ShortName
FROM Customers;
```

Such string manipulations are particularly helpful in formatting customer-facing data, creating identifiers, or performing case-insensitive comparisons.

Date and Time Functions

Date and time functions are essential for querying and analyzing time-sensitive data, such as order history, subscription periods, or project timelines.

- **GETDATE()**: Returns the current system **date** and **time**.
- **DATEADD()**: Adds a specified interval (e.g., **days**, **months**) to a date.
- **DATEDIFF()**: Calculates the difference between two dates.
- **FORMAT()**: Converts date values into a specific display format.

Example: Delivery Estimates and **Age** Calculations

```
SELECT
  OrderID,
  OrderDate,
```

```
    DATEADD(DAY, 7, OrderDate) AS ExpectedDelivery,
    DATEDIFF(DAY, OrderDate, GETDATE()) AS DaysSinceOrder
FROM Orders;
```

This query estimates delivery dates and tracks the days since each order was placed, which is helpful for logistics and customer service reports.

Window Functions

Window or analytic functions operate over a "**window**" or subset of rows related to the current row. Unlike aggregate functions, they do not collapse multiple rows into one. Instead, they enable calculations like running totals, rankings, and comparisons between rows.

- **ROW_NUMBER**(): Assigns a sequential number to rows within a partition.
- **RANK**(): Assigns a rank to rows, allowing for tied values.
- **DENSE_RANK**(): Similar to **RANK**(), but without gaps in ranking.
- **LEAD**() / **LAG**(): Accesses the next or previous row's value.

Example: Ranking Orders and Comparing Sales

```
SELECT
    OrderID,
    CustomerID,
    TotalAmount,
    ROW_NUMBER() OVER (PARTITION BY CustomerID ORDER BY OrderDate) AS
OrderRank,
    LAG(TotalAmount, 1, 0) OVER (PARTITION BY CustomerID ORDER BY
OrderDate) AS PreviousOrderAmount
FROM Orders;
```

This query ranks each customer's orders chronologically and retrieves the value of the previous order—enabling behavioral analysis or churn prediction.

Common Table Expressions (CTEs)

A Common Table Expression (**CTE**) is a temporary result set defined using the **WITH** clause. **CTEs** help simplify complex queries by breaking them into logical building blocks. They improve readability and maintainability, especially when queries involve nested subqueries or recursion.

```
WITH CTE_Name AS (
    SELECT column1, column2
    FROM Table
    WHERE condition
)
```

```
SELECT * FROM CTE_Name;
```

Example: Filtering High-Spending Customers

```
WITH SalesSummary AS (
  SELECT
    CustomerID,
    SUM(TotalAmount) AS TotalSales
  FROM Orders
  GROUP BY CustomerID
)
SELECT *
FROM SalesSummary
WHERE TotalSales > 5000;
```

This query calculates the total sales per customer. It retrieves only those who have spent more than **$5,000**—a practical tool for customer segmentation.

Summary

In this chapter, we delved into Advanced **SQL** Functions, which expand the capabilities of **SQL** beyond basic querying. Mastering these functions enables you to analyze, clean, and present data more effectively—an essential skill in any data-driven discipline.

Section A
Multiple Choice Questions

What does the **DISTINCT** keyword do in a **SQL SELECT** statement?

A. Sorts results alphabetically

B. Removes duplicate records

C. Filters rows by a condition

D. Groups records by column

Answer: B

Which **SQL** keyword allows you to rename a column in the result set?

A. ALIAS

B. AS

C. RENAME

D. MODIFY

Answer: B

The **CONCAT ()** function is used in **SQL** to:

A. Add numbers

B. Combine strings

C. Compare two strings

D. Count characters

Answer: B

Which operator is used to filter data using a pattern in **Oracle SQL**?

A. =

B. LIKE

C. IN

D. MATCH

Answer: B

What does the % symbol represent in the **LIKE clause**?

A. Any one character

B. Exactly one digit

C. Zero or more characters

D. Only uppercase letters

Answer: C

In **LIKE 'S%,'** the query returns:

A. Names ending with 'S'

B. Names containing 'S'

C. Names starting with 'S'

D. All records without 'S'

Answer: C

Which clause is used to remove duplicate rows in a **SQL** query result?

A. REMOVE

B. SKIP

C. UNIQUE

D. DISTINCT

Answer: D

What does the following **SQL** do? **SELECT CONCAT(first_name, ' ', last_name) AS full_name FROM students;**

A. Joins tables

B. Returns student names without space

C. Combines first and last name with a space

D. Select all students

Answer: C

The **||** operator in **Oracle SQL** is used to:

A. Perform division

B. Compare values

C. Concatenate strings

D. Check NULLs

Answer: C

Which of the following will return **NULL** when concatenating with a **NULL** value?

A. **CONCAT()**

B. ||

C. **NVL()**

D. **ISNULL()**

Answer: B

Which keyword ensures all selected rows are **unique**?

A. UNIQUE

B. DISTINCT

C. ONLY

D. FIRST

Answer: B

What does **AS** provide in a **SELECT** statement?

A. Aggregation

B. Aliasing

C. Condition

D. Function

Answer: B

Which **SQL** function replaces **NULL** with a specified value?

A. NVL

B. REPLACE

C. NULLIF

D. COALESCE

Answer: A

What is the default behavior when || is used with **NULL**?

A. Ignores NULL

B. Skips to next value

C. Returns NULL

D. Returns an empty string

Answer: C

What does _ represent in a **LIKE** pattern?

A. Any number

B. Any single character

C. Specific letter

D. Empty space

Answer: B

LIKE '__A%' will match strings with:

A. Starting with A

B. Ending with A

C. A. as the third character

D. A. as first character

Answer: C

Which function joins values with a delimiter in some **SQL dialects**?

A. JOIN()

B. CONCAT_WS()

C. MERGE()

D. UNION()

Answer: B

Which query returns names ending in **'son'**?

A. WHERE name LIKE '%son'

B. WHERE name = 'son%'

C. WHERE name LIKE 'son%'

D. WHERE name IN '%son'

Answer: A

What does **SELECT DISTINCT major FROM students** return?

A. All majors

B. Duplicate majors

C. Unique majors

D. All records

Answer: C

In pattern matching, which wildcard matches any string of any length?

A. _

B. %

C. *

D. &

Answer: B

In LIKE **'T__,'** what is returned?

A. Words starting with T and two characters long

B. Words ending with T

C. Three-letter words starting with T

D. Any word with T in the middle

Answer: C

Which function is used for **NULL**-safe string joining in **Oracle**?

A. CONCAT

B. NVL

C. NVL2

D. CONCAT_WS

Answer: A

How can you rename a column to **full_name**?

A. RENAME column AS **full_name**

B. SELECT column RENAME full_name

C. SELECT column AS full_name

D. MODIFY column TO full_name

Answer: C

Which is a correct concatenation of **city** and **state** with a **comma**?

A. city + "," + state

B. city || ', ' || state

C. CONCAT(city, ', ', state)

D. city . ','. state

Answer: B

Which keyword is used for pattern matching?

A. MATCHES

B. LIKE

C. FIND

D. SCAN

Answer: B

Which clause filters rows based on a condition?

A. ORDER BY

B. WHERE

C. GROUP BY

D. HAVING

Answer: B

Which function returns **NULL** if both arguments are equal?

A. NVL

B. NULLIF

C. COALESCE

D. DECODE

Answer: B

LIKE '___' will match strings of length:

A. Any

B. 1

C. 3

D. 0

Answer: C

SELECT **first_name || last_name** will return:

A. Names with space

B. Names with comma

C. Joined names without space

D. Error

Answer: C

What is the output of **NVL(NULL, 'N/A')**?

A. NULL

B. Error

C. 'N/A'

D. Blank

Answer: C

Which keyword is used to display column headings in queries?

A. TITLE

B. HEADER

C. AS

D. SHOW

Answer: C

Which clause comes after **SELECT** in a query?

A. WHERE

B. ORDER BY

C. FROM

D. GROUP BY

Answer: C

What will **LIKE** '%a' match?

A. Words starting with 'a'

B. Words ending with 'a'

C. Words with 'a' in middle

D. All

Answer: B

Which is not used for string handling?

A. CONCAT

B. LENGTH

C. NVL

D. SUM

Answer: D

Which function returns the first non-null value?

A. NVL

B. COALESCE

C. NULLIF

D. IFNULL

Answer: B

What type of operator is||?

A. Comparison

B. Arithmetic

C. Logical

D. Concatenation

Answer: D

LIKE **'%ing'** will match:

A. Walking

B. Walk

C. Talk

D. Run

Answer: A

Which is the correct aliasing syntax?

A. SELECT name full_name

B. SELECT name AS full_name

C. SELECT AS name full_name

D. SELECT name = full_name

Answer: B

What is the use of **CONCAT_WS()**?

A. Joins values with a separator

B. Sums values

C. Subtracts strings

D. Compares values

Answer: A

What will **SELECT 'Hello' || NULL** return?

A. HelloNULL

B. Hello

C. NULL

D. Error

Answer: C

Which clause can be used with **DISTINCT**?

A. ORDER BY

B. GROUP BY

C. WHERE

D. All of these

Answer: D

Which wildcard matches any one character?

A. _

B. %

C. *

D. #

Answer: A

Which clause is used to name a derived column?

A. BY

B. AS

C. USING

D. WITH

Answer: B

LIKE '%e%' returns:

A. Only names starting with 'e'

B. Only names ending with 'e'

C. Names with 'e' anywhere

D. None

Answer: C

What is the output of **SELECT CONCAT('SQL', NULL)**; in **Oracle**?

A. SQL

B. NULL

C. SQLNULL

D. Error

Answer: B

Section B
Descriptive Questions

Column Aliases

1. What is a column alias in SQL? Provide examples to illustrate its usage.
2. Differentiate between aliasing with and without the AS keyword.
3. Why is aliasing important when performing calculations in the SELECT clause?
4. Explain how aliases improve query readability and maintenance with examples.
5. Can you use column aliases in the WHERE clause? Justify your answer.
6. Write a SQL query using aliases to label columns "Full Name" and "Annual Salary".
7. How do you use aliases when joining multiple tables to avoid ambiguity?

DISTINCT Clause

8. What does the DISTINCT keyword do in SQL? When should it be used?
9. Write a query to find the number of unique cities in a customer's table.
10. Explain the use of DISTINCT with multiple columns and how it affects results.
11. Describe the limitations or performance concerns of using DISTINCT.
12. How would you count distinct departments where at least one employee works?
13. Demonstrate the difference between COUNT(*), COUNT(column_name), and COUNT(DISTINCT column_name) with examples.

Pattern Matching Using LIKE

14. Explain the functionality of the LIKE operator with '%' and '_' wildcards.
15. How can LIKE match names starting with 'R' and ending with 'n'?
16. Write a query using LIKE to retrieve all email addresses from Gmail.
17. Compare pattern matching with LIKE and regular expressions in SQL.
18. Explain how LIKE can be used to perform case-insensitive searches in Oracle.
19. How does the ESCAPE keyword enhance the flexibility of LIKE?
20. Provide a real-world scenario where pattern matching is helpful in data filtering.

String Concatenation

21. Compare string concatenation using || and the CONCAT() function in Oracle.
22. How does Oracle handle NULL values during concatenation?
23. Write a query using || to display a formatted full name: "First Last (City)."
24. What are the limitations of the CONCAT() function in Oracle?
25. Create a SQL query to display a custom employee code in the format: EMP_<ID>_<NAME>.
26. Explain the output of the following query: SELECT 'Hello' || NULL FROM DUAL;

27. Write a query using multiple concatenation operations and explain its result.

Handling NULLs with Concatenation

28. What issues may arise when concatenating columns with NULL values? Provide examples.
29. How does NVL() help resolve issues with NULLs in concatenation?
30. Write a query that shows employee names and phone numbers, using 'N/A' for NULLs.
31. What is the output of SELECT CONCAT(first_name, NULL) FROM employees?
32. Discuss the role of NVL() or COALESCE() in ensuring consistent output formatting.
33. How would you display an address line by combining multiple columns (some of which may be NULL)?

Advanced Query Composition

34. Write a complex query using aliases, DISTINCT, and pattern matching.
35. Demonstrate the use of DISTINCT with ORDER BY and explain the execution sequence.
36. Create a query that lists all customers whose names do not contain the letter 'e.'
37. Design a SQL query that displays student records with aliases for marks, percentages, and grades.
38. Write a query using LIKE to filter product names with special characters like % or _.
39. How can you use DISTINCT with aggregation functions like MAX()?
40. Formulate an SQL statement that returns unique full names from the employee table with title and department.

Conceptual & Real-World Applications

41. Discuss the importance of data cleansing and formatting in retrieval queries.
42. In what scenarios is using DISTINCT discouraged due to performance?
43. How would you design a report query for a dashboard showing distinct customers by region?
44. Discuss how incorrect use of wildcards in LIKE can lead to misleading data.
45. Summarize how combining aliases, DISTINCT, and pattern matching can create powerful reports in SQL.

Section C
Scenario-Based Questions

- **You are managing a customer database** for a retail chain. Write an SQL query to display a unique list of cities where customers live. Add appropriate aliases to make the output readable in a report.
- **A hospital database** contains patient names, contact numbers, and cities. Some contact numbers are missing. Write a query to generate a contact list showing patient names with 'Not Available' where phone numbers are NULL.
- **Design a query** to show the full names of employees (concatenated first and last names) and their departments, ensuring duplicate names are not repeated in the output.
- You are asked to generate a report of all **product names starting with 'S' and ending with 'r'** from an inventory database. Use LIKE and explain your choice of pattern.
- In a **university database**, student names are stored in two columns: first_name and last_name. Using column aliases, construct a query to display full names in the format "Last, First" along with the city.
- You have been given the task of auditing your company's email domains. Write a query that retrieves a list of distinct email domains (everything after the '@' sign) from the employee table.
- You are tasked with cleaning and formatting a **shipping address field** stored in separate columns: street, city, state, and zip. Concatenate them into a single address line using a separator (e.g., comma or dash) and handle any NULL values.
- A marketing manager wants to extract all customers whose names contain the pattern **'__n%'** (two characters followed by 'n' and any number of characters). Explain and implement the query using LIKE.
- You are working on a performance dashboard. Write a query that displays the **total number of unique job titles** and aliases the result as "Unique Roles in Org."
- Suppose your company's database has redundant customer name entries. Write an SQL query using DISTINCT and aliases to **prepare a deduplicated customer list** suitable for sending promotional emails.

Section D
Unsolved Questions

1. What is the purpose of using the **DISTINCT** clause in **SQL**?
2. How do you rename a column in the result set?
3. What is the syntax of the **CONCAT()** function?
4. Explain how the **LIKE** clause is used with patterns.
5. What is the difference between % and _ in pattern matching?
6. Write a query to select all unique job titles from an employee's table.
7. How do you concatenate first and last names in **Oracle SQL**?
8. What will be the result of using **||** with one **NULL** operand?
9. Write a **SQL** query to find all customer names that end with the letter '**a**'.
10. How do aliases improve the readability of **SQL** queries?
11. Which function helps handle **NULL** values while concatenating strings?
12. Write a **SQL** query that shows full names as "**Last, First.**"
13. Create a query using **DISTINCT** with multiple columns.
14. Explain what happens when **DISTINCT** is applied to multiple columns.
15. Write a query to return all rows where the city name starts with 'San.'
16. How do you use **LIKE** to find names containing the letter 'e'?
17. Write a query using **CONCAT()** to display employee full names with a hyphen **(-)** between them.
18. What are the possible issues with using too generic aliases?
19. How do you write a query that returns only cities with five-character names?
20. What is the default behavior of **SQL** when handling **NULLs** in concatenation?
21. Write a **SQL** query using **NVL()** to replace **NULL** department names with "**Unknown.**"
22. How is **||** different from **CONCAT()** in **Oracle SQL**?
23. Can **DISTINCT** be used in combination with **ORDER BY**? Explain with an example.
24. Write a query to select students' full names, but only those who live in 'Texas.'
25. How do you identify duplicate values in a column?
26. Explain the importance of using wildcards correctly in pattern matching.
27. Write a query to fetch names starting with 'A' and ending with 'n.'
28. What is the output of **LIKE '__a%'**?
29. Describe a use case where aliasing is essential for clarity in a complex query.
30. What is the result of this query: **SELECT 'SQL' || NULL FROM dual;**?
31. Can aliases be used in the **WHERE** clause? Why or why not?
32. Write a query that selects customer names containing exactly six characters.
33. How do you display results as "**First Last (City)**" using **CONCAT()** or **||**?
34. Write a query using **DISTINCT** to show unique combinations of first_name and city.
35. What happens if you omit the AS keyword while aliasing a column?
36. What does **LIKE '_o%'** return in a names column?

37. Write a query that shows departments with names containing the word "**Sales**".
38. Can **DISTINCT** be used with aggregate functions? Justify your answer.
39. How do you filter values using **LIKE** in a case-insensitive manner?
40. What role does aliasing play when using functions like **CONCAT()** or **NVL()**?
41. Write an **SQL** statement to return employees with **NULL** in the phone number field.
42. Construct a query that lists all students with names not starting with '**A**.'
43. Write a query showing all values from a column with the third letter 'e'.
44. How do you ensure accurate formatting when using concatenation with **NULLs**?
45. Explain the usage of **NVL()** in string-based operations.
46. What's the difference in result between using || and **CONCAT()** with multiple values?
47. Describe a situation where duplicate rows are acceptable in output.
48. Write a query that combines two columns with a comma and space separator.
49. How does **Oracle SQL** handle **NULLs** differently than other databases in string functions?
50. Create a query to display customers whose names do not contain the letter 'a'.

INDEX